BIGGEST

AND

smallest

Written by
Camilla de la
Bédoyère

FIREFLY BOOKS

A FIREFLY BOOK

Published by Firefly Books Ltd. 2011

First printing

Publisher Cataloging-in-Publication Data (U.S.)

De la Bédoyère, Camilla.
  Biggest and smallest / Camilla de la Bédoyère.
[32] p. : col. photos. ; cm.
Includes index.
Summary: About the biggest and smallest animals on the planet, with facts and photographs.
ISBN-13: 978-1-55407-805-9 (pbk.)
ISBN-10: 1-55407-805-9 (pbk.)
1. Body size — Juvenile literature. 2. Animals — Juvenile literature.
I. Title.
590 dc22   QL799.3.D425 2011

Library and Archives Canada Cataloguing in Publication

A CIP record for this book is available from Library and Archives Canada

Published in the United States by
Firefly Books (U.S.) Inc.
P.O. Box 1338, Ellicott Station
Buffalo, New York 14205

Published in Canada by
Firefly Books Ltd.
66 Leek Crescent
Richmond Hill, Ontario L4B 1H1

Picture research: Starry Dog Books Ltd
Designed & edited by Starry Dog Books Ltd
Consultant: Dr Gerald Legg, Booth Museum of Natural History, Brighton

Printed in China

Developed by:
QEB Publishing, Inc.
3 Wrigley, Suite A
Irvine, CA 92618
www.qed-publishing.co.uk

Picture credits
Key: t = top, b = bottom, l = left, r = right, c = centre,
FC = front cover, BC = back cover.

A = Alamy, C = Corbis, FLPA = Frank Lane Picture Agency,
G = Getty Images, IQM = imagequestmarine.com,
NPL = Nature Picture Library (naturepl.com),
PL = Photolibrary, PS = Photoshot, S = shutterstock.com.

FC l S/ © Kletr, FC r S/ © Al Mueller; BC bl S/ © Eric Isselée, BC tl, tr, br S/ © Picsfive.

1l S/ © Christian Musat, 1r S/ © Eric Isselée; 2 S/ © Mogens Trolle; 3t S/ © Peter Wollinga; 4l IQM/ © Peter Batson, 4r S/ © pandapaw; 5l S/ © Eric Isselée, 5r Dr Daniel Kronauer, Harvard University; 6t S/ © Torsten Lorenz, 6b S/ © Christian Musat; 7t S/ © Mogens Trolle, 7b S/ © Andreas Meyer; 8 S/ © Stephen Inglis; 9t S/ © Alan Merrigan, 9b PL (Juniors Bildarchiv); 10t S/ © Dominique Capelle, 10b S/ © Attila Jándi; 11 PL (OSF)/ © Rafi Ben-Shahar; 12 PS (NHPA)/ © Martin Harvey, 12b S/ © Dennis Donohue; 13t A/ © David Osborn, 13bl A/ © Lee Dalton, 13br S/ © Eric Isselée; 14t PS/ © Gerald Cubitt, 14b S/ © Nickolay Khoroshkov; 15t S/ © Jaana Piira, 15b S/ © Jerry Sharp; 16t S/ © fivespots, 16b IQM/ © James D. Watt; 17t NPL/ © Nick Garbutt, 17b IQM/ © Scott Tuason; 18c IQM/ © Jez Tryner, 18b FLPA (Minden Pictures)/ © Norbert Wu; 19t IQM/ © Peter Parks, 19b IQM/ © James D. Watt; 20b C/ © Michael & Patricia Fogden, 20-21 G/ © Peter David; 21t S/ © KRCrowley, 21b S/ © Eric Isselée; 22t IQM/ © Johnny Jensen, 22b S/ © Morten Hilmer; 23t S/ © Ewan Chesser, 23b S/ © Le Do; 24-25 C/ © Denis Scott, 24b IQM/ © Peter Parks; 25t S/ © Lijuan Guo, 25b IQM/ © Peter Parks; 26c S/ © Peter Wollinga, 26b S/ © Eric Isselée; 27 S/ © worldswildlifewonders; 28l S/ © Debra James, 28r S/ © Photobank; 29tl S/ © Linn Currie, 29tr S/ © Martin Maritz, 29cr S/ © Katrina Brown, 29br S/ © Tischenko Irina; 32 S/ © Morten Hilmer.

The words in **bold** are explained in the glossary on page 30.

Contents

Big and Small

Life is tough in the animal world. Sometimes being big can help you to survive, and sometimes being small works best.

More **complex animals** with big brains, such as elephants, tend to be bigger than the simpler animals, such as starfish and spiders.

The no. 1 tallest animal **RECORD BREAKER** is the ...

GIRAFFE

Giraffes are the tallest animals in the world. Their great height helps them to reach into trees and feed on leaves that smaller animals can't reach. Giraffes can be 20 feet (6 meters) tall.

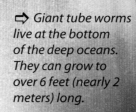

➪ *Giant tube worms live at the bottom of the deep oceans. They can grow to over 6 feet (nearly 2 meters) long.*

Who's cleverest?

There are no hard-and-fast rules in the **animal kingdom**. Little pygmy marmosets grow to just 6 inches (15 centimeters) long, but they are very clever monkeys. Giant tube worms are thirteen times larger than pygmy marmosets, but they have no proper brain at all.

➪ *Little pygmy marmosets can leap and dart between trees, using their tail for balance. They live in the rainforests of South America.*

ACTUAL «« SIZE »»

Driver ants are giants in the bug world. The queen is 2 inches (50 millimeters) long. She grows so big because she has to produce millions of eggs each month. The world's smallest ants (*Carebara* ants) measure just 0.03 inches (0.8 millimeters) long.

Driver ants with their queen

in 1 2 3 4

Is Big Best?

What is best about being big? For one thing, it means most hunters will think twice before attacking you.

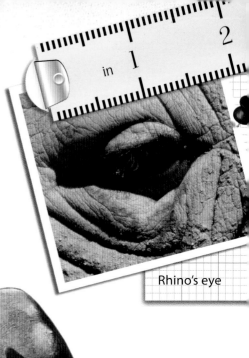

⬇ *White rhinos are actually gray. They live in Africa and can grow to 13 feet (4 meters) long.*

Rhino's eye

6

ACTUAL « SIZE »

Rhinos have surprisingly small eyes for their great size. These grazers rely more on their sense of smell to detect danger.

⬇ *Lions usually hunt animals that are smaller or weak. When they hunt in a group, they may attack larger prey.*

A rhino is the size of a small car and is covered in thick skin. It is simply too large for most big cat **predators**, such as cheetahs or lions. If a big cat did attack one of these mighty beasts, it would stand a good chance of being squashed underfoot and stabbed by the rhino's horn.

Advantages of size

Being big makes some animals, such as lions and bears, better hunters—they are able to defeat other, smaller animals more easily. Being large has another advantage, too. It helps a body to stay at a steady temperature, and this allows the animal to save energy. Animals that have a tiny body, such as the common shrew, lose heat quickly.

The no. 1 biggest land animal **RECORD BREAKER** is ...

SAUROPOSEIDON

Although big bodies can support big brains, it isn't always the case. The dinosaur Sauroposeidon was the largest land animal ever to have lived. It stood an incredible 59 feet (18 meters) tall, but its head was very small in relation to its body.

Small to Survive

Most of the world's animals are much smaller than us. There may be as many as 30 million species, or types, of animals. Of these, at least 9.8 million are smaller than your hand!

Invertebrates are animals without backbones, such as worms and beetles. Backbones and bony skeletons hold a big body up. Since invertebrates don't have this support, they are mostly small.

⇐ *Most praying mantids are long, green and glossy— just like leaves. They can hide among plants, and pounce onto other small animals.*

ACTUAL «« SIZE »»»

Goliath bird-eating spider

Most spiders, even small ones, are equipped to kill their prey with deadly **venom**. One of the biggest spiders is the Goliath bird-eating spider, which is about the size of a dinner plate! Its legspan can be nearly 12 inches (30 centimeters).

in 1 2 3

A neat package

Being small—whether you are a mini moth or a tiny turtle— means you may have some advantages over bigger beasts. You can probably hide better, you don't take up much space, you can eat less, and you don't have to spend years growing big enough to mate and have young.

⬇ *The stinkpot turtle is one of the smallest turtles in the world. It measures about 2 to 5 inches (5 to 12 centimeters) long, and makes a foul smell when it is scared!*

9

Curious Cousins

When a male African elephant walks up to you, there is no doubt that you are face to face with one of nature's giants.

An elephant can measure 30 feet (9 meters) from trunk tip to tail tip and weigh more than 13,200 pounds (6000 kilograms). This makes it the world's largest land animal.

Fur in the family

Strangely, the elephant's closest cousin seems to be a furry little **mammal** called a hyrax. There is not much of a family likeness!

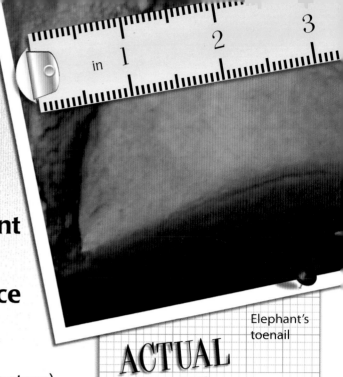

Elephant's toenail

ACTUAL «« SIZE »»

Elephants can talk to each other using their feet. They make low rumbling noises, which other elephants feel as vibrations that travel through the ground and into the soles of their feet.

Telltale bones

Scientists think that elephants and hyraxes are related because the bones in their feet and teeth are very similar. They also both live very long lives— elephants usually to about 60 years and hyraxes to 15 years.

← *Rock hyraxes live among rocks and like to sunbathe.*

⇦ *African elephants are the largest of all elephants. They have much bigger ears than Asian elephants. An elephant's tusks are teeth that can grow to 10 feet (3 meters) long.*

Feathered Friends

⇩ Ostriches live in the grasslands of Africa.

Birds come in all shapes and sizes, from the mighty ostrich to the miniature bee hummingbird.

12

All birds have feathers, but not all of them fly. The world's largest birds are built for speed on land. They are simply too heavy to fly.

The no. 1 biggest owl **RECORD BREAKER** is the ...
EURASIAN EAGLE OWL

The Eurasian eagle owl is the largest of all owls, with a record breaking wingspan of 6.5 feet (2 meters). The females are bigger than the males.

Long legs

An ostrich stands about 6.5 feet (2 meters) tall. When it runs, it can cover more than 16 feet (5 meters) in one giant stride. Its small wings are no good for flying, so when an ostrich senses danger, it has to run fast or kick its attacker.

⇦ *Albatrosses fly long distances over the ocean to reach land, where they make their nests and lay their eggs.*

ACTUAL «« SIZE »»

The bee hummingbird measures just over 2 inches (51 millimeters) long, including its tail and bill. It is the world's smallest bird, and is easily mistaken for a bee. Weighing a fraction of an ounce, it is so light that you wouldn't feel it resting on your hand. The whole bird is about the same size as an ostrich's eye!

Bee hummingbird

Ostrich's eye

Expert gliders

Albatrosses have huge wings, useful for gliding on warm **air currents** high in the sky. The wandering albatross has the largest wingspan of any bird. Its wings measure 138 inches (350 centimeters) from tip to tip.

13

in 1 2 3 4

Social Climbers

Apes, monkeys and lemurs are primates. They like to live in family groups, and their bodies are perfect for climbing trees, where they find fruit to eat.

⇧ *Pygmy mouse lemurs rarely come down from the trees. Their large eyes help them see well in the dark.*

⇦ *Large male gorillas are called silverbacks, because their fur turns gray as they age. One silverback is in charge of each gorilla family, and he protects them.*

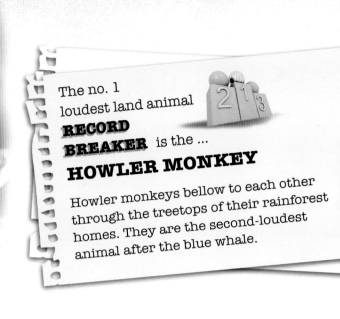

People used to think that gorillas were a type of monster, but now we know they are gentle giants—and apes, like us. Gorillas are the largest primates. They are so big that they spend most of their time on the ground, but even the "big daddies" occasionally climb high up a tree to fetch ripe, tasty fruit. If they feel threatened, gorillas use their great size to scare away other animals, and humans, too.

Nifty movers

The pygmy mouse lemur is the world's smallest primate. It is only 2.4 inches (6 centimeters) long, but its tail adds another 5 inches (13 centimeters). Pygmy mouse lemurs live in the forests of Madagascar. Being small means they can scuttle swiftly through branches at night, searching for insects, flowers and fruit.

ACTUAL «« SIZE »»

Gorillas have hands that are very similar to ours. Each large hand has four fingers, a thumb and fingernails. Gorillas can use their hands to grip, hold, twist and open things, too.

A gorilla's fingernail

Scary Reptiles

Millions of years ago, reptiles were the largest animals ever to have lived. In the long run, being big did not help them survive.

Today's reptiles are much smaller than the dinosaurs. But that doesn't mean you would want to come face to face with them! The Komodo dragon is a large lizard. It can grow to nearly 10 feet (3 meters) long and is famous for being fast on its feet, aggressive and having a deadly bite.

The no. 1 scary reptile **RECORD BREAKER** is the ...

RETICULATED PYTHON

Snakes are reptiles, too. The largest snake is the reticulated python. The longest one ever found measured more than 30 feet (9 meters) long. This snake eats birds, rats, stray cats, goats and even monkeys.

⇦ *Komodo dragons are the world's heaviest lizards. They hunt reptiles, wild pigs and deer. They even eat their own young.*

⬇ *Saltwater crocodiles can swim far out to sea, hunting for prey to eat. Their massive jaws hold dagger-like teeth that can grow up to 5 inches (13 centimeters) long.*

ACTUAL ≪ SIZE ≫

Unlike its big cousins, the pygmy chameleon is just 1.4 inches (35 millimeters) long when fully grown, including its tail. Imagine how tiny it must be when it emerges from its egg!

Pygmy chameleon

in 1 2

Watch out!

Crocodiles and alligators can grow to a great size, even reaching 23 feet (7 meters) in length. Nile crocodiles normally hide underwater, waiting for their prey. They are so big and strong, with huge teeth and jaws, that they can attack and devour zebras and **wildebeest**.

Big Appetites

Animals that eat large meals often eat only occasionally, but those with smaller appetites spend most of their time feeding.

Gulper eels live in the ocean depths, where food is scarce. They grow to 6 feet (1.8 meters) long, but most of that is mouth! A gulper eel can open its jaws so wide that it can swallow a fish as big as itself. Its body stretches to fit the food in. The eel can last for weeks without another meal.

⇩ The remains of this gulper eel's last meal can be seen as a bulge in its body.

18

The no. 1 small to big **RECORD BREAKER** is the ... **SUNFISH**

The sunfish grows up to 13 feet (4 meters) across, but a baby sunfish is smaller than a pea. This animal holds the record for the greatest difference in size between the adult and its young.

All mouth but no bite

Whale sharks are the biggest fish in the world. Their mouth can measure 60 inches (150 centimeters) across, but they don't use it to gobble up other marine monsters. Instead, they swim along with their mouth open, and water and small animals flow in. Their prey is mostly plankton—animals no bigger than your little finger.

ACTUAL «« SIZE »»

Plankton are tiny animals and plants that float or swim in the ocean. Some are so small they can only be seen with a microscope. They are an important source of food for many other sea animals.

Plankton

in 1 2 3

⬆ Whale sharks can grow to about 40 feet (12 meters) long. They spend most of their time swimming and feeding.

Mighty Mates

At mating time, being big and strong can be a real advantage for male animals.

In many species, males have to fight one another to get a mate. The females choose males that look big, because it means they are more likely to have healthy young.

Fearsome horns

A male Hercules beetle can grow up to 7.5 inches (19 centimeters) long, including its huge horns. It uses these either for fighting rival males, or for scaring them away. The females are so much smaller that scientists once thought they belonged to a different species.

⇦ Male Hercules beetles display their large horns to each other. The smaller one may decide to walk away from a fight.

The no. 1 mighty mate **RECORD BREAKER** is the ...

MOOSE

Moose, or elk, live in cold, northern parts of the world. Males can grow twice as large as females and their antlers have been known to span a record 6.2 feet (1.9 meters).

Shrinking male

Not all males outgrow their partners. Some grow into them! A male anglerfish is tiny and can sneak up on a female. He bites into her flesh and stays in place, to mate with her, for the rest of his life. His body gradually shrinks and he takes **nutrients** straight from her blood.

⇧ In the deep, dark oceans, where anglerfish live, finding a mate is hard. So when a male anglerfish finally finds a female, he never lets go of her.

ACTUAL «« SIZE »»

Hercules beetle

The horns of a Hercules beetle are made from a tough material called chitin. The top horn grows from the beetle's body and curves downward. The other one grows from its head and curves up. Together they look like huge biting jaws.

in 1   2   3   4

Body Bits

Why do animals grow strangely big, or small, body bits?

A body part may grow extra large if it has a very important job to do. Walruses, for example, have overgrown teeth, or tusks, which they dig into slippery ice to help pull themselves along. Male walruses also use their tusks to fight one another.

⇧ *Cavefish live in darkness, so they do not need to be able to see.*

22

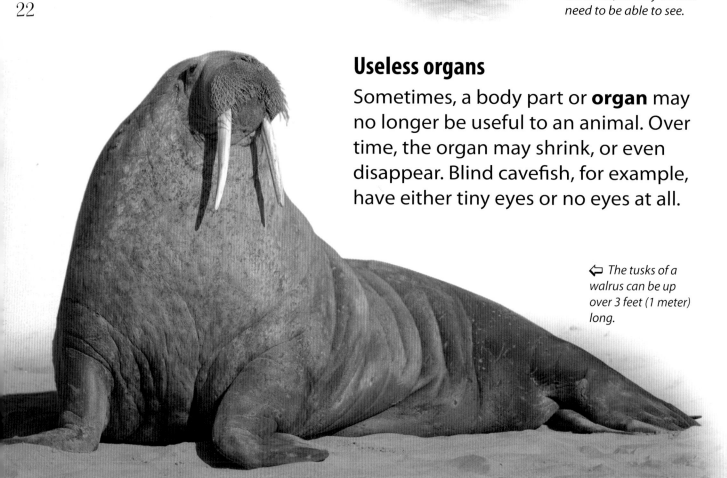

Useless organs

Sometimes, a body part or **organ** may no longer be useful to an animal. Over time, the organ may shrink, or even disappear. Blind cavefish, for example, have either tiny eyes or no eyes at all.

⇦ *The tusks of a walrus can be up over 3 feet (1 meter) long.*

⇨ *Tarsiers hunt at night. Their huge eyes help them find prey, such as insects, bats, birds and snakes.*

Eyes like saucers

Animals that are active at night often have very big eyes, which give the animal better vision. The tarsier's eyes are huge in relation to its body size.

23

ACTUAL «« SIZE »»

Dragonflies have eyes that take up most of their head. Each eye contains thousands of tiny lenses that produce a single image in the dragonfly's brain.

eye

Dragonfly

in 1   2   3

Marine Extremes

The oceans are home to the biggest and smallest of creatures.

The salt in the world's seas and oceans makes the water **dense**. This means it can support the weight of heavy animals, even if they don't have a bony skeleton—for example, octopuses and jellyfish.

⬇ *Blue whales spend the winter in cold polar waters, feasting on krill. They eat very little, or nothing at all, during the rest of the year.*

ACTUAL «« SIZE »»

Krill

Krill are small marine creatures that are closely related to prawns, crabs and lobsters. Billions of them can live in a single group, or swarm. Fish and whales travel long distances to feed on swarms of krill.

6   5   4   3   2   1   in

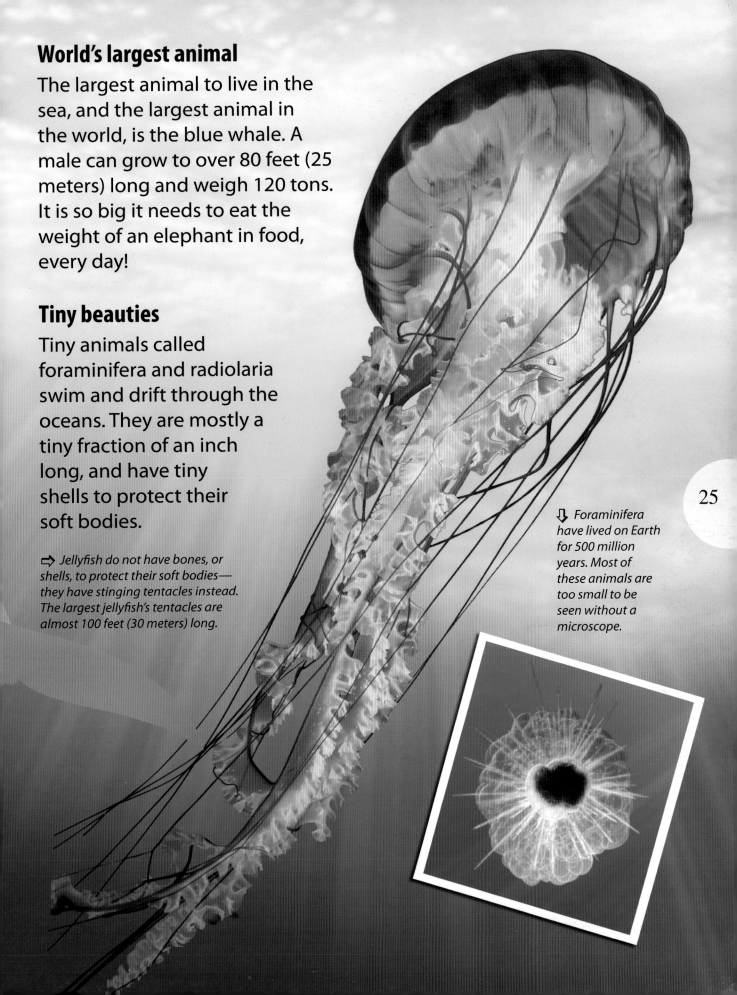

World's largest animal

The largest animal to live in the sea, and the largest animal in the world, is the blue whale. A male can grow to over 80 feet (25 meters) long and weigh 120 tons. It is so big it needs to eat the weight of an elephant in food, every day!

Tiny beauties

Tiny animals called foraminifera and radiolaria swim and drift through the oceans. They are mostly a tiny fraction of an inch long, and have tiny shells to protect their soft bodies.

⇨ *Jellyfish do not have bones, or shells, to protect their soft bodies— they have stinging tentacles instead. The largest jellyfish's tentacles are almost 100 feet (30 meters) long.*

⇩ *Foraminifera have lived on Earth for 500 million years. Most of these animals are too small to be seen without a microscope.*

Jungle Giants

Jungles, or tropical rainforests, are home to a huge range of living things of all shapes and sizes.

Rainforests are very special **habitats** that provide a home for lots of different species of living things because they offer plenty of food, shelter, water and warmth. About 80 percent of all insect species live in rainforests.

Big and bold

When an immense Atlas moth flutters through the dappled shadows, it can easily be mistaken for a bird. Another jungle giant is the Philippine eagle, which is so vast and fast that it can catch a lemur as it leaps between trees.

ACTUAL « SIZE »

Small poison arrow frogs don't have to hide from predators because their skin contains a deadly toxin, or poison. One lick of their skin is enough to kill a predator. Their bright colors warn predators to stay away.

Poison arrow frog

⇧ The Atlas moth has an enormous wingspan. It measures up to 11.8 inches (30 centimeters) from wing tip to wing tip.

4   3   2   1   in

Magnificent tail

Male quetzals catch the eye of possible mates by flashing their bold colors and tail feathers, which can reach over 3 feet (1 meter) long!

⇧ *The spiky feathers on a male quetzal's head are called a crest. Females do not have crests, or long tail feathers.*

Little Goes Large

In the big world of little animals, ganging up often works well. When they work together, animals can make mountains!

Tiny termites live in groups, or colonies, of up to five million. Their underground tunnels can extend 150 feet (45 meters) deep, and the mounds they make can be nearly 25 feet (7 meters) high.

⬇ *Termites are called social insects because they work together to build their enormous mounds. They feed on wood and plants, as well as fungi, which they grow inside the mound.*

The no. 1 animal structure **RECORD BREAKER** is ...

THE GREAT BARRIER REEF

Australia's Great Barrier Reef is the largest structure ever built by animals. It is more than 1,200 miles (2000 kilometers) long. The tiny **polyps** that are building it started work about 18 million years ago!

Safety in numbers

Red-billed queleas are the most numerous of all birds—there are billions of them in Africa. Queleas live in giant groups, called flocks, and this gives them protection from predators. When feeding on crops, a flock can strip whole fields in hours. One quelea flock may contain a million birds, or more.

⇐ *Red-billed queleas are small birds, but when they are flying in a giant flock they look like a dark storm cloud.*

⇓ *Honeybees are social insects. Up to 100,000 of them may live in a single nest.*

29

ACTUAL « SIZE »

Honeybees on a honeycomb

Animals that live in colonies communicate with each other. Honeybees tell one another where to find the best flowers by performing a **waggle dance**!

in 1 2 3 4

Glossary

Air current Warm air is lighter than cool air, so it rises and moves across the sky. This is called an air current.

Animal kingdom The group of living things that contains all of the animals on Earth.

Complex animal An animal that has a body with limbs, such as legs or wings, and organs, such as a brain.

Dense Materials that are dense contain particles (tiny bits of stuff) that are closely packed together. Salty water is more dense than fresh water.

Habitat The place where an animal or plant lives.

Mammal An animal that has fur and feeds its young with milk.

Nutrient Found in food, nutrients contain the goodness that animals and plants need to live and grow.

Organ A part of the body that has a special job to do. The stomach, for example, digests food.

Polyp A soft-bodied animal that lives in the sea. It makes a stony substance around its body that collects and, over a long time, makes a coral reef.

Predator Any animal that hunts another animal to eat.

Primate A type of mammal with a large brain. Primates include humans, monkeys and apes.

Species A type of animal or plant.

Tropical rainforest A warm forest where there is heavy rainfall all year long.

Venom A type of poison made by some animals, including various snakes, frogs and spiders. Venom is used to kill prey or to cause pain to an attacker.

Wildebeest A kind of antelope, also known as a gnu.

Waggle dance Honeybees waggle their bodies, and walk around in circles. The way they do this 'waggle dance' shows other bees where to find flowers with sweet nectar to eat.

Index

Notes for Parents and Teachers

Here are some ideas for activities that adults and children can do together.

◆ The "Actual Size" panels will help children to understand many of the measurements in the book, but others need to be seen to be believed! Use a tape measure to explore the larger sizes quoted.

◆ Go on a bug hunt together. Gardens, parks and woods offer lots of opportunities to watch insects and other invertebrates in their natural environment. Take a magnifying lens, a small ruler, a sketchbook and a pencil to record your observations. Don't touch the bugs, though, and watch out for those that sting!

◆ Use weighing scales to find other things that weigh the same as a bee hummingbird.

◆ Many of the animals in this book can be seen in zoos and wildlife parks, or in natural history museums. If you are able to visit one of these places together, try and find the largest and smallest examples of types of animals. For example, find the largest cat or the smallest reptile.

◆ Encourage children to think how an animal's size might help the animal to find food or a mate, or avoid being eaten.